IN PRAISE
OF
SCOTTIES

A BOOK OF CELEBRATION

To Alistair, Lyn + Flora
Enjoy the Scotties en this book!
Ann x

ANN HART BILLINGHAM

Supporting STECS
Registered charity number 275666

ISBN 9780957459328

Published by Ann Hart Billingham February 2014
Printed in the UK by BUZPRINT, Bury St. Edmunds, Suffolk,
England

ACKNOWLEDGEMENTS

Firstly, thank you to all the Scottie owners who took the time to share their lovely Scotties with me. Without you this book could not have been created. Thank you for your enthusiasm and encouragement.

My thanks also go to:

STECS - for endorsing this fund raising venture, in particular, Karl Hahm, for your advice and encouragement and Joy Gower, for marketing support.

KLODJAN – for working your magic with the page numbering.

BUZPRINT - David Fuller, for putting up with my endless questions pre-production and for continuing to teach me about the technicalities of printing. Your knowledge and patience is very much appreciated.

MY FAMILY - for once again enduring the chaos that surrounds us all when I am creating and producing a book.

~~ A Special Thank You to ~~

All the Scotties who are featured in this book. You make this book special and unique – a real *'Scottie Treasure'*.

Ann

to Maeve, Murphy and Maud

*for all the Scottie love and joy you give us
and for being the inspiration for this book*

FOREWORD

I have had some success over the past couple of years with publishing fundraising books for local charities. These have all had a food theme and contained home-cooked recipes donated by local communities. However, as passionate as I am about food, this does not match my absolute and unwavering passion for Scottish Terriers.

I met my first Scottie in 1969 when my mum brought *Bonnie* home to join our family. She was a remarkable dog, stoical and so much fun and I have many happy childhood memories of growing up with her.
It wasn't until much later, in 1995 that I became a Scottie owner in my own right when I brought *George* into my life. I have owned Scotties ever since and we now have a 'Scottie Family' with *Maeve, Murphy* and little *Maud*.

What better way to feed my passion for Scotties than to produce a book for Scottie lovers, at the same time supporting the U.K. based Scottie charity STECS – Scottish Terrier Emergency Care Scheme - for rescuing and re-homing Scotties.

I hope you enjoy looking at and reading about the lovely Scotties in this book. It really is a book of celebration!

Ann Billingham

'It's a Family Affair'

Featuring Maeve Billingham, Madge and Pip Moore.   Photo by Ann Billingham

CONTENTS

SCOTTIE PERSONALITIES

SCOTTISH TERRIER
Origin ~ Scottish Highlands : Popularly known as the 'Scottie'

Admired, respected and loved for its loyalty and bravery, the Scottish Terrier has been held in high regard for centuries. Every Scottish Terrier has its own unique personality but there are distinct behavioural and genetic traits and characteristics which are deeply ingrained in these independent little dogs. These include a robust, muscular body, large feet and nose, powerful jaws and a thick coat designed to repel rain and provide warmth in a harsh climate.

This sturdy little terrier is no pushover and refuses to be intimidated. I have often heard the Scottie described as 'a big dog in a small package'. This little 'tyke' with the short legs and long head has the courage of a German Shepherd and thinks he is the size of a Great Dane.

Scotties are adventurous, have pluck and intelligence and are quick, alert and sturdy, with keen hearing and excellent eyesight. Dignified and bold, self-assured and feisty, loving and playful. These unique little dogs embody passion and energy and evoke it in those around them.

This loveable rogue possesses the *elite factor* that attracts a very select crowd. Sometimes described as aloof, each one has their own unique soulful character.

I believe that Scotties meet life as they find it with a mellow understanding. They are very adaptable and can adjust easily to changing situations. Scotties are extremely loyal to their family. If you love them, respect and treat them with dignity, they will love and protect you to the end.

The Scottie enjoys walks, playing fetch with a ball, food (!) and nothing more than quiet family nights snuggled up warm in the comfort of their own home.

They are a class act and if you are like me, once you have given your heart to a Scottish Terrier, it will remain true and steadfast to this breed for a lifetime.

Ann

SCOTTS

ON

PARADE

PART 1

MADGE, PIP AND PETER

Madge and Pip are strong 'Berrybreeze' girls, passing through their middle aged years.
They are beautiful, resolute and sometimes artful...

...They liaise...

'That's a good Scottie gap in the hedgerow!'
...We'll sit here and gaze at the sheep across the valley!'

...Peter is our darling boy; he is only a year old and looks up to them,
his giddy head thinks only of play and friendship.

'They'll stay', they think we are the alpha leaders! Delusional, we are wafty like the distant haze hanging over Compton Down with its long grass and tangled brier.

The Downs change to Dorset's old broad leafed woods; mulch under paw, sniffing for rabbits and scouting for squirrels their long snouts hunting.

...Atavism

Small, excitable Aberdeen wolves morph into Constables soft green: and the loved Scotties are caught by the doting camera.

November 2013

Madge, Pip and Peter's owners: Lucy, Stephen and Ru, Dorset, England

MOLLY AND BUNTY

Molly, 7 from Brockenhurst, Hampshire is a strong-willed, determined and headstrong Scottie with a soft centre. She is playful and mischievous, understands every word we say and communicates with us with meaningful looks. Dislikes: fireworks, balloons and lawn mowers. Likes: playing chase, eating and snoozing. *Bunty*, 6 from Gillingham, Dorset is friendly, trusting and adventurous. She loves cuddles and tummy rubs and is always ready for fun! Dislikes: water, traffic and big dogs. Likes: watching television, tug games and squirrels.

They visit a nursing home regularly where my Mum and many of the other residents have Alzheimer's and struggle to communicate. They love seeing Molly and Bunty, their eyes light up and they smile with pleasure as our two Scots do their rounds saying hello (surreptitiously hovering up the floors as they go!). Molly and Bunty are angels (usually), have enhanced our lives enormously and we love them both to bits.

October 2013

Molly & Bunty's Owners*: Sylvia and David Stooke, Wiltshire. England*

HAMISH

Hamish is 5 years old and enjoys life at Chelsea (a beachside suburb of Melbourne), Victoria Australia.

In 2012, Hamish had 48 hours to live when Scottie Rescue Australia rang and asked us if we would be interested in a male wheaten coloured Scottie. His owners had a vets appointment to have him put down because of his aggression. Having killed a fox on their farm and maimed a koala which died, they were worried about their 7 month old baby.

One look at Hamish and we fell in love. Although we were in fear and trepidation at what Hamish would be like when we walked him on the beach each day, we hoped we could help him. Hamish had never been allowed indoors but he adjusted very easily into being an indoor dog. He wakes us up by his "Scottie talking" each morning!

After 6 months and never having been let off the leash, his aggression towards other dogs was getting worse

It was time for a dog behaviourist. We were taught how to train him and play games. The trainer suggested changing his food, only giving him treats for being good and instead of the chain choker collar, a normal one. We also had to put some pebbles in a plastic jar and if a dog came near and Hamish looked as if he was going to attack - shake it. He improved a little, but three months later he slipped out of his collar and headed for a group of dogs and their owners. *I freaked out.* Next thing, Hamish is sitting in the middle of the dogs wagging his tail, sniffing their bottoms and smiling. Since then he has enjoyed running around in the sand dunes and playing with all the other dogs on the beach. He has a perpetual smile on his face and is very obedient. *He is a totally different dog!*

He gets excited seeing himself and other Scottie dogs on the computer videos and also enjoys animal shows on the television.

We feel it is such a miracle to get him and see the changes in him........and we love him so. My husband, who didn't want another dog, is besotted with Hamish too and said "HE IS THE BEST DOG WE HAVE EVER HAD".

Thank you Scottie Rescue Australia
October 2013

Hamish's owners: Mary and Ted Barker, Victoria, Australia

FREDDIE

Fred, 5½ months, lives in the Granary Barn at Elton on the Hill in Nottinghamshire. His best friend is Buddy, a Cockapoo who lives next door. They romp and play every day for 10 agonising minutes as Fred hangs on to Buddy's ears and is whisked around the garden.

Fred is brave and very gentle. He has not yet learned to wag his tail back and forth - it goes round and round like a windmill! He will sit and give paws for treats and mostly will come when he's called. He's quite tiny and I secretly hope he stays that way. He loves the TV and frequently looks around the back it of the set when someone or some animal goes off screen.

We lost our big Scottie, George, last October at 11 years. I didn't think any dog could take his place but little Fred has created his own special niche and it's a wonderful place to be.

October 2013

Freddie's owners: Richard Lindsley & Damian Burke, Nottinghamshire, England

TUCKER

Tucker (m) came to us from a local breeder here in Clearwater, Florida, where he lives with me and my husband. He's a handsome wheaten Scottie with light colouring over his shoulders that look like "angel wings" - but don't be fooled, he's NO ANGEL! His favourite thing is to chase lizards! Fearless, he dives under bushes, hopping across the yard like a lamb. On walks he barks at dogs and anything with wheels. At two, he's more settled and I can get a little cuddle from him despite the fact that he's a daddy's boy. He's bright, curious and comes running at the crinkle of a bag just in case there's a treat in it for him. He's assertive enough to push open a door but hides from the vacuum.

A funny little guy, who makes our home so complete.

October 2013

Tucker's owner: Pam Nuss, Florida, USA

HAMISH

Hamish is a 3 month old black Scottish Terrier and came to live with us in Northallerton, North Yorkshire when he was 9 weeks old. Hamish was the only boy in a litter with 6 sisters and was born in Leek in Staffordshire. Hamish is a very happy, friendly dog who loves meeting new people...he just doesn't like them to go home! He loves to play, especially with his tug toy but he also loves to play fetch with his ball. In the 4 short weeks that we have had Hamish he has learned so much, he now asks to go out when he needs to go toilet and is very good at giving you his paw when a treat is on offer. He is a very inquisitive puppy; he even likes to watch TV. He really is a joy to have and brings much happiness into this household.
November 2013

Hamish's owner: Vanessa Hodgson, North Yorkshire, England

BARNEY

Barney, who is now 5, arrived with us in May 2010 from STECS. He was 18 months old then and from Gloucester. He had blotted his copybook by being 'noisy' at his previous owners. He turned out to be the most energetic Scottie we have had and loves to bark at practically anything. In fact we are convinced that he has canine Tourette's, if this is possible. His name was quickly extended to Barney T. Rubble and this is on all his documents now. Everyone agrees that he is well named.

He just loves everyone and all other animals, especially women visitors. At some time in his past some kind lady must have given him a treat from her handbag, as now we have to warn all female visitors to keep their handbags securely with them because he can open and check the contents in a flash.

November 2013

Barney's owners: Joan and Robin Lawrie, Northumberland, England

HAMISH AND HOLLY

Hamish is our shining star! He was our first Scottie and is a lovely cuddly and very determined little boy. He was diagnosed with liver cancer following a biopsy in 2010 when he was 11yrs old. It could not be treated and they gave him two months to live. Naturally we were devastated, but he didn't hear them and here he is, over three years later and still doing well aged 14½.

The loves of his life are two little girls, Holly aged nearly 10yrs and Lucy Locket his little cream Burmese cat, aged 15yrs. Sadly Holly was also diagnosed with cancer in May this year, but she is still going strong and she, Hamish and Lucy are inseparable. They have shorter walks nowadays but for most of their lives they have had long walks through our fields and woods.

Lucy hated to be left out and would rush out to follow us all along the walk, bumping the two dogs and leaping over them, rushing ahead then dashing up and down trees keeping us all entertained.

When Holly first came to our home as a little puppy we put a gate at the bottom of the stairs so Lucy could get away from her because she would chase Lucy all over the house.

One night after a short while I found that Lucy was not in her usual sleeping place on our bed so I went downstairs to find her curled up with Holly beside the Aga! They still cuddle up there together on their special little cashmere rugs - a treat for the elderly pets who we love so much.

November 2013

Hamish and Holly's owners: Jacqui and Roger Collier, Suffolk, England

Hamish and Holly with Lucy

JOCK

Jock is 11 years old and we got him from a notice board in a local supermarket aged 6 months.

He was living with a family with young children, who were unable to manage him. He has been a delight to have and is a much loved member of our family.

He is totally spoilt, has his two walks every day and also has what we call a "Jockey Day" regularly, where we take him to his favourite haunts.

He has travelled with us to France and loves nothing more than being towed behind me on my bike, in his specially adapted trailer!
November 2013

Jock's owners: Sue and Ken Unsworth, Lancashire, England

ANDY, HOANTEG AND HEATHER

Andy is my first Scottie (f) and she is 8 years old. Hoanteg (m) and Heather (f) are both 1yr. They live with my Westie,
Morwenn (f), who is 4.
We live in Brittany near the sea in Fouesnant. They all love going for a walk on the beach at the port and Hoanteg and Heather like going to dog shows. They all play together, they are very happy and they are really funny. There are 2 cats living in the house also and sometimes they sleep together... or they playfully chase each other!
They all sleep on my bed and I love them so much. They have a good life, are never alone and they make me feel so good and happy. It's a LOVE STORY!
November 2013

Andy, Hoanteg and Heather's owner: Christelle Le Roux, Fouesnant, France

JAZZ AND BENI

Born in Moscow, Russia, I now live in the Netherlands. I have had Scotties all my life and these funny, sweet gentlemen have always been close to my heart. Now I have 2 Scottish Terriers. Benedikt (Beni) is a white Scottie who I rescued from the Ukraine because he had Scottie cramp and nobody wanted him. Beni is very independent, very sweet and is the boss of the house! My other Scottie is Jazz. He came from the Netherlands – nothing wrong with him. He is also very sweet and cannot stay home alone without jazz music on the radio.
Beni and Jazz were born on the same day, 24th December 2010, but in 2 different countries. 24th December is my birthday also! They live with me and my husband in The Hook of Holland and they love to run on the beach and swim in the sea.
November 2013

Jazz and Beni's owner: Natalia Shchegolkova, Hook of Holland, Netherlands

LULU

Lulu was born on New Year's Day 2012.

She is a brindle Scottie and came to live with me and my Westie when she was 8 weeks old. Sadly, we lost my Westie due to old age earlier this year, so it's just me and Lulu now. I first met her when she was 4 weeks old at her breeders in Essex, where I also met her mother, a wheaten Scottie, and her father, who was brindle.

Lulu is very friendly, always pleased to see people and enjoys her daily play, rain or shine, in our local park, just enjoying herself. However she will often have a spat when lead walking in the street upon meeting another terrier. I didn't know the meaning of the word 'stubborn' until entering 'Scottie world'. Westies were pretty good at exhibiting this trait too, but not a patch on the Scottie!

It must be a Scottie thing - Lulu loves watching dogs and cats on television and displays her pleasure often by barking and jumping up at the TV set. She is also an avid fan of Wimbledon tennis - watching the ball, (not quite so good at retrieving her own ball though).

Lulu has loads of character and she loves a cuddle. I love her to bits!
November 2013

Lulu's owner: Kathie Taylor, South East London, England

OSCAR

Oscar is 6 years old. He lives in Dundee and was born in Aberdeenshire in Scotland. He is very loyal and very strong in guarding his house, which seems to be the way Scotties are. He prefers the company of Iain and follows him all around the house and garden. This is great company for Iain as Oscar is always there, never asks for anything and never misbehaves. However there is lots of Oscar to go around, so when the family are all in one room Oscar does his best to give everyone a bit of his attention. Like most dogs he can sense when someone is low, upset or ill and provides his passive comfort which is always successful in cheering us up. When he's not thinking of others and cheering us up, he likes to watch any television programme with animals, 'Pet Rescue' being his favourite.
November 2013

Oscar's owners: Pearl and Iain Rennie, Dundee, Scotland

BETH

Beth is my black Scottie aged 4 years. She came to us from a breeder near Eastbourne, UK at only 8 weeks old. She shares our house with our 6 ½ year old Westie, Ralph.

Since arriving she has regularly attended a dog obedience class (more of a social gathering for humans as well as canines) and has achieved her gold kennel club GCDS award. She can be quite nervous in busy towns and feels much more at ease in a field. She is a very good house dog and loves peace and quiet in her cosy bed. She is rather picky as to which other dogs she takes a shine to. She can sit for hours looking out of the patio windows for squirrels. She is rather petite but super-fast on her feet.

A game of ball goes down a treat!
November 2013

Beth's owner: Bekka Smith, Surrey, England

TINK AND HARLEY

Tink is my girl. Here she is on the left, sporting her 'winter look'. She is 3 yrs. old and very playful.

Tink has a new best friend, Harley. Here he is on the right, being cute, as only Harley can.

Harley is just 4 months old. He is boisterous, never quits eating and if he doesn't get his gravy bones, he likes to eat slippers!

They love chasing each other and running around the garden together. They also love walks in the local park, although Harley is a typical Scottie – so stubborn. He just lies down and doesn't move if he doesn't get his own way!

November 2013

Tink and Harley's owners: Maedea and John Carson, County Armagh, Northern Ireland

ROSIE

Rosie is our black Scottish Terrier. She is 6yrs old and joined our wee family 2yrs ago at the age of 4. Rosie is a wonderfully loveable and cuddly fur baby and we call her our 'Intrepid Forager' as when out for a walk, if there is something smelly, Rosie will roll in it...eeek! Her best friend is Ruby our Westie and together they are affectionately known as 'The Ladies'. Rosie is such a bright and loyal wee Scottie and brings so much laughter and smiles. The only thing that Rosie doesn't like is fireworks and has been known to jump from the floor onto the dining room table in one leap! Do not be fooled by their wee legs as they are expertly hidden tightly coiled springs that enable them to jump high and run very fast. To be owned by a Scottie is a wonderful thing and I consider myself a very lucky lady.
November 2013

Rosie's owner: Lana Warrender, Inverness, Scotland

HARRY

Introducing Harry - aka 'Harry McPotter'. Harry is the proud owner of Amanda, Paul, Katie and Emily. Harry came to us from a breeder at the age of 11 months. He fitted in from day 1 with Barney our other Scottie who has now sadly gone to Rainbow Bridge. Harry is a perfect little gentleman who only wants to please, when in the house. Out on walks, he thinks he is 10 ft. tall and wants to put everyone in their place. He goes to a doggy play group once a week and they lovingly refer to Harry as the BOUNCER! He keeps everyone in check.

He is my friend and confidant; we all love him so very much. It would be a very empty life without a Scottie and a very empty house without Harry.

November 2013

Harry's owners: Amanda and Paul Dinning, Tyne and Wear, England

BRUCE

Bruce is a 2 ½ year old black Scottish Terrier. Being very fit and active, he keeps his owners walking up to 50 miles a week, particularly loving his beach walks.

Bruce is very difficult to tire out; he will not give up and even did an 11 mile charity walk without any effort.

He loves going to doggie day care twice a week and has lots of friends there. Apparently he will not let them rest, constantly wanting to play.

Bruce is a real mammy's boy and every night without fail he finishes his day on the settee for cuddles and with his favourite naughty snacks of cheese and rich tea biscuits!

November 2013

Bruce's owners: Karin and Dougie Johnson, County Durham, England

JOCK AND MAGGIE

Jock, aged 15 yrs. is a silver brindle. He came to live with us and Jess almost 4 years ago. Jock is one of the most gentle Scotties I have owned (9). You can do anything with him except look into his mouth. He walks among the birds in the garden and they don't even bother with him or fly away. He plays nose ball and enjoys gardening (digging) with his dad. He also enjoys walks and meeting the neighbours but I think his most enjoyable pastime is being in the company of humans. When there are a group of people or at a party, you will always find Jock in the centre of the group looking up as if he is taking it all in. To summarize - Jock he is the most loveable Scottie you could hope to have.

Maggie, aged 6 yrs. is jet black. She came to us after Jess passed away 3 years ago, as a companion for Jock. She was a skinny, scared little thing with a big bald patch and big, very sad eyes. Although still quite frightened of strangers, Maggie has come on fantastically. She is quite funny at times, as she growls and backs up when people come into the house.

Eventually she pokes them with her nose to be petted. She loves long walks and racing around the circumference of the garden. She loves to be cuddled and is very obedient. She also thinks she should go everywhere with you. If you give her a telling off, her ears go straight out (like Gizmo) and she sticks to the floor. She is such a lovely dog.

We feel so fortunate to have them and would not be without them.

November 2013

Jock and Maggie's owners: Jean and Archie Hill, Kirknewton, Scotland

JOCK MCPHEE

Jock is an 8 year old black Scottish Terrier. I chose him as a puppy from the Kilkenny Kennels in Oxford and collected him at 8 weeks old.

He is a multi-faceted, larger than life character that brings a smile to our faces every day. He loves his routine. Jock remains upstairs in the morning, waiting for me to go down. Then he comes downstairs with me. He has his dental stick, goes into his garden and likes to look over the low wall at the passers-by, enjoying a good bark at the post man. Jock also loves going for walks. These are all the things he likes to do up until Scott gets home. Then it's time to play 'fetch the ball'.

Jock loves cuddles, sleeping on his back, his arm pits tickled, his grandma and children, long walks and splashing around in the mud or streams and playing - but all in his own good time!

In return he laughs, talks and is affectionate, loyal and strong. Jock is sensitive to our moods and an absolute fur ball of joy.

November 2013

Jock's owners: Ruth and Scott Farrell, Yorkshire, England

JIMMY AND JESS

When I was little there was a communal family Scottie who came to visit and I made the decision then that when I was bigger I would have one.

That one turned into two - Jimmy & Jess, who are both 5 years old. Jimmy came first and I always worried he would be lonely - then came Jess.

Jess rules the roost and Jimmy is very protective of her and me. Jimmy doesn't like other male dogs and thinks he can take on the world. Both are very stubborn and won't do anything they don't want to do.

I wouldn't have it any other way - life is never boring when they are around. They have their own personalities which are both so different. I can't imagine my life without a Scottie. Maybe time for number 3!

November 2013

Jimmy and Jess's owner: Karen Gill, Ayrshire, Scotland

MAC AND DOUGAL

Mac is 4 years old and a very typical black Scottie. He does let his hair down sometimes but this is his usual pose. Doug, Dougal or DOUGLAS (!) is a wheaten and the polar opposite to Mac. He doesn't do *the sitting thing*. He is into everything good and bad; he has bucketful's of naughtiness and does not walk anywhere. He is Mac's son from his first litter 18months ago. I think secretly Mac does like him really.

November 2013

Mac and Dougal's owner: Jan Hankin, Cornwall, England

NESSIE

As we write this short biography Nessie is 14 days away from her sixteenth and a half birthday. We brought her home in August 1997 and the following weekend she was very poorly. We were extremely concerned about her and sat up all night nursing her. At 4.00 am we heard the news that Princess Diana had died in a car crash. We will therefore never forget what we were doing when Diana died. Nessie recovered and has enjoyed 16 healthy years.

Nessie in 2010 with her Scottie family – Florrie, Hamish and Sporran

From 8 months old she established herself as top dog, a position she retains today. Nessie currently lives with Sporran (f), a black Scottie who is 9 yrs., Hazel (f), a black Jack Russell x Staffie who is about 14 yrs. and Billy (m), 8 yrs. - our daughter's rescue white Jack Russell. Nessie loves holidaying in Scotland and her favourite place is the beach at Dornoch. The photo of her stealing the snowman's carrot was taken at Kildrummy Castle, Aberdeenshire. Indeed, one of her hobbies is stealing vegetables and she once ate a whole cucumber that we had left in the back of the car!

November 2013

Puppy Nessie

Nessie, aged 16 yrs.

Nessie's owners: Jean and Karl Hahm, Cleveland, England

'It's a Love Thing'

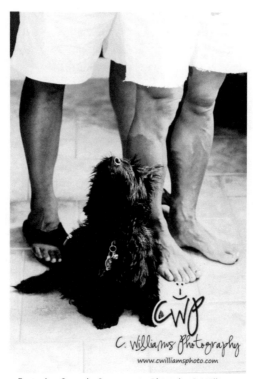

Featuring Corrado Castro.   Photo by C. Williams

SHARING LIFE WITH A SCOTTISH TERRIER

I was always a 'Boxer' man. When I was younger, my family and I owned Boxers and I still love the breed deeply to this day.

When I first met Ann, it was therefore with some concern that I was greeted with the news that she was a 'Scottie' girl.

However, once I met George my fears were quickly allayed; I knew this was a breed I would love.

I was going to call this piece *'Owning a Scottie'* but soon realised what a ridiculous title that would have been. For herein lies their secret, the thing that creates the kind of adoration that is everywhere within this book: one does not *own* a Scot, one shares life with them in a mutually beneficial partnership, built on equity, trust and love. A relationship that is collectively far greater than the sum of all its parts, as all good relationships should be.

My great mistake was thinking of Scotties as *small* dogs, with all the characteristics associated with that description. Scotties are *big* dogs in every way that matters. They are fiercely loyal and yet massively independent, wilful but sensitive, caring and playful but also protective. I think one of the qualities I admire in them the most is their courage.

Scotties are happy to share their space with you, so long as you acknowledge that it is *their space*!

So, sharing your life with a Scottie? I can wholeheartedly recommend it.

Leslie Billingham

SCOTTIE RULES!

Scotties are independent little dogs who seem to have their own set of rules by which they live. They are quite attached to their belongings and appear to live by this set of 'property laws' ....

If I like it, it's mine
If it's in my mouth, it's mine

If I had it a little while ago, it's mine
If I can take it from you, it's mine

If it's mine, it must never appear to be yours
If it just looks like it might be mine, it's mine

If I saw it first, it's mine
If it's edible, it's mine

If you have something and you put it down,
it's mine
If I chew something up, all the pieces are
mine

If I get tired of it, it's yours
If I want it back, it's mine!

SCOTTS

ON

PARADE

PART 2

AMY

My Scottie x Westie, Amy is an extremely happy, laid back girl. She is 3 years old and we live in Derbyshire.

In winter, Amy loves to play with her Kong squeaky balls after tea. In summer, she loves to be outside from morning to night. On her walks, Amy loves to chase squirrels in the local park and cemetery. She has a best friend in an Akita called Holly.

I have supported the UK Scottie charity - STECS since getting my first Scottie Shona in 2000.

November 2013

Amy's owner: Jacqueline Cater, Derbyshire, England

Amy with her best friend Holly, the Akita

MEG AND TESSA

Northorne Summer (Meg) and Kenxiam Solar Wind (Tessa) are mother and daughter and they live on our farm at Ottery St Mary in East Devon, England. Meg was a wedding present from my husband in 2006. I was 48 years old when we got married and told him that I wanted a baby for a wedding present... so he was very relieved to find out that I actually wanted a puppy! I am an asthma sufferer which was one of the reasons why I chose a Scottie, as they hold onto their coats. Plus, I had always wanted a Scottie.

Meg, who has a black/brindle coat, was bred in North Devon and is an incredibly intelligent and loyal dog. She is pest control manager on the farm and can go from a standing start and catch a rabbit. Meg loves to be out on the farm with me and supervises the care of the chickens, pigs and horses.

Tessa was born in 2011 and is black apart from a few white hairs in her tail. Her sire was Champion Berrybreeze Reckless Eric who lives in Somerset with Clair Chapman of Berrybreeze Scotties. Eric has passed on his good looks and lovely silky coat to his daughter. Tessa likes nothing better than to curl up on my lap in the evenings and insists that I keep stroking her head, nudging my hand if I stop.

My Scotties are family pets and are dogs with big personalities.
They are fabulous to have around and are loved by everyone who meets them.
Their picture was taken in March 2011, when Tessa was seven months old.
2013

Meg and Tessa's owner: Mrs Ann Brown, Devon, England

STRIKER

My love for terriers began in my childhood. Striker is a brindle Scottie, who was born on March 29, 2011 in Cumming, Georgia. He now resides in North Carolina. 'Striker' is his call name. His registered name is 'Riverbend Strikes It Rich @ Eroglen'. His pedigree goes back to 'Bardene Bingo' who was imported from overseas to live here in the United States of America.

Striker is a show dog and we are working on getting his American Champion title.

He is such a wonderful Scottie with a lot of energy and he loves giving 'Scottie kisses' to the girls. My little boyo is full of life and antics. He is a great comfort and an entertainer also.

Scottish Terriers are *one of a kind* and Striker knows he rules!
November 2013

Striker's owner: Brenda S. Bosse, North Carolina, USA

MORAG

This is my beautiful, 6 month old, black/brindle Scottie called Morag. She lives with me in Whitby, North Yorkshire and came to me when she was 8 weeks old from a breeder in Selby.

Morag loves going out on walks and meeting new people and other dogs and she LOVES food. She has a passion for anything on two wheels, chasing stray leaves blowing around in the wind and sees joggers as an invitation to a race!

At the end of the day, she likes nothing better than to lie on my chest and watch the television, especially Top Gear and Doctor Who.

I cannot imagine my life without her in it.

November 2013

Morag's owner: Chloe McDermott, North Yorkshire, England

PEPPER AND FALA

Pepper 2yrs (f) and Fala 6.5 months (f) live in the valley of Senghenydd, South Wales. They are black Scotties. Pepper came to live with us at 8 weeks and soon made friends with Monty, our Scottie cairn cross. Fala is the daughter of Pepper, one of five beautiful Scotties in the litter. She still sees her brother Jock on a daily basis as he only moved a few doors away. Pepper and Fala are family pets and share our house with Monty (dog) and 3 cats. They all love to play together which can sometimes be a bit hectic. They both love to be out walking or running and love big open spaces, which is lucky because we are surrounded by mountains.

Pepper and Fala love to paddle in the sea and roll in the sand on the beach. If Monty doesn't run, Pepper will encourage him by nipping at his back legs! Most of all, both Fala and Pepper love cwtches (cuddles). They are both intelligent dogs as they understand Welsh and English and can follow instructions in both. When they get excited they dance on their back legs and like to 'give you five'.

At the end of the day they love to cwtch up together for a nap.
November 2013

Pepper and Fala's owner: Samantha Hopkins-Giles, Senghenydd, South Wales

RODY

My previous Scottie Sam died from lymph cancer when he was 8 years old. My heart was broken and I didn't want to have any other dogs. But after 3 months, my good friend Natalia brought me this wonder from Moscow.

I named him Rody. He is very sweet and also has a real Scottie character. He is very gentle with people but he wants to be the boss among other dogs. I have to save him by taking him up into my arms and then all the other dogs jump up and they are hanging off my arms!

Rody and I walk a lot in the forest and we enjoy every moment.

I am 2m 05cm tall and he is 1 meter long and people enjoy seeing us because we make a really funny couple.

November 2013

Rody's owner: Kees Hoornik, Hook of Holland, Netherlands

ALFIE

Alfie (we're guessing 10-11 years old) lives in Northern Ireland. He is a rescued black Scottie and arrived here 5 years ago. Picked up as a stray by the dog warden, he was in the pound with demodectic mange and was going to be pts. With our vets treatment he improved and has never looked back.

Alfie is choosy who he welcomes, some people get a sniff and wag of the tail or he hops onto their knee, others he might just totally ignore.

We don't think Alfie had a great start in life, possibly not very well socialised and so out on walks he might greet a submissive female with a sniff but some off lead dogs get screamed at (his way of saying go away).

Alfie loves his walks, paddling in the sea and digging holes in rock pools, but enjoys cuddles at the end of the day.

November 2013

Alfie's owner: Elaine Davidson, County Londonderry, Northern Ireland

JOCK

Jock is 6 ½ months old and he lives with me in South Wales. He is a black Scottie with a wheaten chin and lives with four cats. Jock loves to play and run and cause mischief and chew anything he can find. He enjoys spending time with his mother Pepper and his sister Fala and sees them on a daily basis. Jock loves to spend time with his best friend Gizmo (cat) and they cause mischief together. Jock enjoys running on the beach and loves his mountain walks. He also loves just cwtching (cuddling) up on the sofa with me. Jock is loved by all who meet him and loves visiting where I work and having a big fuss made of him by staff and residents, who all love seeing him.
November 2013

Jock's owner: Emma Louise Hopkins, Senghenydd, South Wales

MAEVE, MURPHY AND MAUD

Introducing: Maeve 5yrs. (*f*), Murphy 3 yrs. (*m*) and Maud 4 months (*f*).

They are all black Scotties and came to live with our family as puppies at 8 weeks old. Maeve, Murphy and Maud are family dogs. They welcome visiting dogs and guests into our home and are very friendly. When they meet other dogs outside on their walks they are a bit choosier and you can never quite predict whether they will wag their tails or scream at them! They love their garden all year round, be it basking in the sun, playing fetch, enjoying a game of football or simply routing around in the bushes. Maud, at her young age takes great pleasure leaping from one flower pot to another, with little regard for the plants within. They love to sit outside listening to neighbourhood sounds, watching birds fly overhead, barking at planes and helicopters and daring the local cat to enter their domain.

They enjoy going for lovely walks and paddling in water. They are Scotties with a zest for life and by day, like to sit at the window watching the world go by. At night they love nothing better than snuggling up with us on the settee.

Most of the time though, they are busy doing what Scotties do and our lives wouldn't really be quite the same without them.

December 2013

Maeve, Murphy and Maud's owners: Ann, Leslie, Aiden and Findley Billingham, Essex, England

CORRADO

Corrado is our pride and joy. Marcel and Jennifer Castro of the United States are his proud human parents.

Corrado was born February 26, 2012, in North Carolina in the USA. He is a black male brindle.

My dream since I was 5 years old was to have a Scottie of my own. When I laid eyes on 'Jock' in *Lady and the Tramp*, I knew this was the only dog for me. Marcel and I drove 14 hours round trip to get our little 'boy' when he was 5 weeks old. Life has never been the same since. Corrado is the beginning and ending of every moment of our lives. He has the heart of an angel. He loves his walks, his car rides, his 'Poppa Time', his home cooked meals every single day and his constant hugs and kisses.

Corrado brings out the best in each of us. He may be small in stature but his presence is momentous.

November 2013

Owners: Jennifer and Marcel Castro, North Carolina, USA

CASPAR

Caspar, who is 5, lives with his people in Cheshire.

Caspar came to live with us at 8 weeks old and has been in charge of our house ever since.

Caspar is fascinated by the television and finds there is nothing better than watching a favourite show accompanied by the odd crisp or two. He works off these extra calories by playing his favourite game 'chase', around the living room every night. He has an aversion to letters being delivered by the postman and enjoys giving any correspondence a Caspar 'stamp' with his lovely teeth.

After being diagnosed with chronic hepatitis two years ago, he has to have plenty of check-ups, blood tests and scans and he is medicated daily. However, this has not dampened his wonderful spirit, as he still loves being with his family, acting like a big baby at home and an absolute terror while out on walks.

November 2013

Caspar's owners: Wendy, Alan and Ailsa Peate, Cheshire, England

JAMIE

Jamie is 6 ½ years old. He is our 10th Scottie. He is quite small for a Scottie. He is dark brindle in colour and has very short legs. Jamie is a very determined little chap and does not have to speak for us to know what he wants. He loves carrots but he does not like baths!
His best friend is Kipper, a wheaten terrier. Jamie loves to go on walks and enjoys sniffing. He loves visitors, especially family.
Jamie is a typical Scottie.
November 2013

Jamie's owner: Shelagh McLean, Northumberland, England

WILLIAM

William is 2 ½ years old, is black/brindle and he resides with me in Florida, USA.

William came into my life at a critical time. I had just recently had to have a Scottish Terrier named Brodie put to sleep after 11 years. I had owned Scotties for almost 20 years and decided I couldn't be without one.

While helping at the 'Scottish Terrier Rescue of the Southeast' booth at an event in Florida, I noticed many dogs having great fun doing lure coursing. I entered William in 4 fun runs that day. William has gone on to become the first Scottish Terrier in the USA to earn an advanced title in that event.

William and I have been most recently involved in conformation shows. He is presently half way to his Championship status.

William often accompanies me when I go places. It's always a treat for he and I to meet new people. I am amazed at how many people claim they have never met a Scottish Terrier in real life.

November 2013

William's owner: Skip Sodano, Florida, USA

PEPPER AND BONN

Pepper 2yrs *(f)*, Bonn 3 months *(m)* live in North Lanarkshire in Scotland.

They are black Scotties and came to live with my family as puppies – they are family dogs. Pepper is currently doing a great job of demonstrating good behaviour to wee Bonbon and has been most accommodating to her new buddy. We are very proud of her. Bonbon finds fun in everything and has brought us lots of laughter.

Both dogs love having visitors at home and are very friendly to other dogs and people on outside walks. Pepper's nickname is McPuddles as she is particularly fond of them – the muddier the better – with Bonbon wading along behind her. Puppy training is great fun and Pepper is delighted to demonstrate and receive training treats in return. After an exciting walk, they love nothing more than snuggling up with the family.

November 2013

Pepper and Bonn's owner: Michelle Carroll, North Lanarkshire, Scotland

FRAZER

Frazer is a black Scottie who is 11 months old. He came to me at 8 weeks from a local breeder. He is my first Scottie, indeed first dog and so we are learning together (often the hard way!). He is bright and learns quickly but, as is the independent Scottie nature, he doesn't always want to do as he is told. He has been described as grumpy but loveable and so he is perfect for me. He is very sociable and loves to play with humans and fellow canines alike, but has recently found that geese aren't so keen to play with him! He is full of life and tackles new experiences head on with enthusiasm – and a little bounce! He loves nothing better than to end his busy days with a large chew next to me on the sofa.
November 2013

Frazer's owner: Fiona-Jane Cook, Bedfordshire, England

JOC

Joc is 11years old and lives in Harrogate, North Yorkshire.

He was born in Llandeilo, West Wales and was given to me as a Christmas present when he was 9 weeks. We lived in Pontypridd, South Wales until he was 4.

He adores humans of every variety but is very choosy when it comes to canines! He lives for his walks – especially when the walk involves a tennis ball or stick chasing.

One of the strangest 'Jocisms' is just after he has something nice to eat, he hunts for a sock and then spends ages finding the best place to bury it! He has done this all his life.

Joc's favourite food includes poached salmon, roast beef and custard cream biscuits.

He has got me through some of the most difficult and dark times during the last 10 years; he just knows when I need him and is always there for me.

Joc has recently battled testicular cancer. He is doing so well and I am immensely proud of him.

Joc brings absolute joy to whoever comes into contact with him. He is as strong willed, independent and territorial as any Scottie you'll find! Most of all he is my companion and my best friend.

November2013

Joc's owner: Julie Evans, North Yorkshire, England

NESSIE

Nessie is 5 years old and lives in the rural hills of Derbyshire.

She is a big black Scottie who came to live with us at 10 weeks old from a lady who had a surprise litter of puppies after her old Scottie Max had his wicked way with Poppy her new dog.

From an early age Nessie loved water even trying to get in her water bowl for a paddle. She loves to swim in any water and all our holidays and days out involve visits to the beach. She loves to run as fast as she can into the sea and there is no catching her if she can smell the sea air. She also loves her frizz bee and can jump quite high for a Scottie. When she does stop, she is a loving cuddly girl who loves to snuggle up with you in the evening

November 2013

Nessie's owner: Joanne Phillips, Derbyshire, England

JENSEN

My name is Jensen. I am nearly two and am also known as Glengracie Formula One. I live with my twin sister Betty, my Mom Fudge, my granddad Alfie and my little cousin Jessie. We live in the countryside in South Lincolnshire with our breeders Angie and Mel. I am a very lively lad. I suppose I live up to my name and travel everywhere at great speed.

I enjoy the company of people and love to sit on someone's knee, but my favourite thing is dog showing. When mum gets the stuff ready I am there waiting excitedly to get into the car.

November 2013
Jensen's owner: Angela Beckton, South Lincolnshire, England

MY SCOTTIE FAMILY

REGGIE AND BAILEY

Reggie is fun loving guy who is 2 yrs. old. He is very affectionate for a Scottie. Reggie had a tough go and we almost lost him several times, He is doing awesome since being diagnosed and treated appropriately in Guelph Animal Hospital in Toronto Canada. He got very ill after his vaccinations at 4 months old. He was put on steroids and developed Cushings disease from them. After a long detox off the steroids and surgery in June 2012, Reggie finally looks and acts like a 2 year old! At last he can play and have fun after all the suffering. He loves to hunt and chase rabbits. He especially loves his brother Bailey, who we adopted in May 2013. They are best buddies as well as brothers and they act like twins. Reggie and Bailey have helped each other heal their physical and emotional wounds.

Bailey is 5 yrs. old. We saw him on Facebook for adoption shortly after we joined the group – 'Scottish Terrier Health'. He was scared, shy and broken hearted when we met him. I loved him from the moment I saw him. It took a lot of love and time to bring him out.

He had the saddest eyes and would cling to Reggie. When Reggie was sick he would cling to me. After Reggie's surgery, Bailey kept kissing Reggie and looking out for him while he was healing. He would chase people away and protect Reggie. After about a month his eyes started glowing! He loved playing and walking with Reggie every day in the park or on the beach. Bailey loves to hunt and actually taught Reggie to be a better hunter.

Watching Bailey & Reggie together makes everyone laugh. They are truly like twins! They mirror each other's every move.

It is a both a blessing and a miracle to me every day to see and watch both of them play and be happy. They always have huge Scottie smiles and wagging tails. They recently won third place at a Halloween costume party and had a blast!

November 2013

Reggie and Bailey's owner: Sparkle St Marie, Las Vegas, Nevada, USA

RUFUS AND MISHKA

Rufus (male) and Mishka (female) both aged 2 years old, live in Staffordshire with their owners.

I fell in love with Scotties over 25 years ago when I got my first Scottie. I didn't want one initially! They looked like bad tempered old men when cut properly, with their beards and eyebrows. Now I would not be without them. These are Scotties 4 and 5. They have beautiful temperaments, very loyal, intelligent, oh yes and stubborn too! They love to meet other dogs on their daily jaunts. Rufus loves to swim. Mishka can't get out of the wet quick enough. My Scotties love to sit outside on the patio surveying their 'estate'. They are both fascinated by animal programmes. At the end of the day though, they love a cuddle and sleep.

November 2013

Rufus and Mishka's owners: Sue and Chris Trueman, Staffordshire, England

LEONARD

Sex: Male
Colour: Brindle
DOB: 06.03.2011
Age: 2 ½ years
Place of Birth: North Yorkshire
Lives: West Yorkshire since he was an 8 week old pup

Personality: Cheerful, enthusiastic, loyal, mischievous, fiercely independent, inquisitive and affectionate

Most attractive quality: Knows his own mind!

Hobbies: Chasing squirrels, deer, cats, hens, birds....; burying bones; sleeping; helping with vegetable preparation by eating broccoli, peppers, carrots and green beans

Loves:	Ball Action!
	Snow
	Sea
Hates:	The Groomers
	Rain
	Mornings

Best Friend: Aunty Phoebe (aka the cat!)

Naughtiest habit: Running upstairs and eating the cat food
Most annoying habit: Selective deafness
Funniest habit: Doing 'The Walrus' every night whilst we're watching TV
Best part of the day: 'Whirler' treat time! (for being a good boy when dishwasher is being loaded)
Perfect day out: Trip to the seaside
Biggest regret in life so far: Eating too much seaweed whilst on holiday in Wales recently
Thinks: Walks are vastly overrated
Dreams of: Having longer legs
Ambition: To be a 'Good Boy'
November 2013

Leonard's owners: Katie and Simon Papp, West Yorkshire, England

HAMISH, BONNY AND ISLA

Here I am with Bonny. I am on the right.

And here is puppy Isla

I'm Hamish and I am 7yrs old. I live with my family in Hampshire. I like to think of myself as cool, loyal and devilishly handsome.

My biggest passion in life is football, closely followed by a tummy tickle. It was just me, the cats (brought for my amusement!) and my folks for a while.

Then 3 years ago my Mum brought Bonny home. No one consulted me, let's say, I was less than impressed. It was like an arranged marriage for a while, but now we are inseparable. We fight like most couples; she throws me out of bed, steals my treats and toys but we always lick and makeup. Over the years we have been blessed with puppies. Maud Billingham in this book is one of our babies. Life was pretty near perfect for a while and then Isla happened!

A wheaten Scottie, Isla is 19 weeks old and still persists on hanging off my beard. Puppies these days have no respect for their elders – the youth of today!

November 2013

The three of us!

Hamish, Bonny and Isla's owner: Kelly Warmington, Hampshire, England

POLLYANNA

This photo features Pollyanna (CH Charthill Quick Silver ROMX) with her first litter of puppies. From left to right are Lucas, Darby, Pollyanna, Alexa, Trump and Camilla. Lucas & Camilla are now AKC Champions and Trump is a Grand Champion.

2010 was a historic year for Pollyanna due to her achievements in the whelping box and she became AKC's Top Terrier Dam as well as the recipient of STCA's Brood Bitch of the Year award.

Pollyanna is now retired enjoying a much deserved life as a couch potato with us, a champion daughter, 2 of her 6 month old grandkids and a male English import.

At home, our Scotties run in a pack and Pollyanna always has the last word.

We absolutely adore sharing our lives with this very special lass!
November 2013

Pollyanna's owner: Robin Geppert, Missouri, USA

BARLEY

My name is Barley Simms and I am 4 yrs. old. I am a Wheaten Scottie and live with my STECS rescue Scottie brothers Oliver and OJ and Ronan the Westie. My passion in life is agility. I started agility training a couple of years ago. Now most of my weekends are taken up travelling and taking part in agility shows. Along with mum, dad and brothers we pack the car up and head off for a fun packed day. I have progressed from a grade 1 agility dog to a grade 5. I am only one win away from becoming a grade 6 then I will be competing with some of the best agility competitors in the country. I am known on the agility circuit as the Scottie 'Queen of Agility' and I always promote how great Scotties are and what a great charity STECS is.
November 2013

Barley's owners: Gill and Paul Simms, Cleveland, England
(Re-homing reps. for STECS)

MAGGIE

Hello, I am Maggie. I am a black Scottie and am 8 yrs. old. I live with Maisie who is a Westie and the same age as me. Mum bought us from a pet shop when we were 10 weeks old. I am very loving and playful, but an older lady now, so not that interested in toys anymore. Mornings, I like to sit looking out of the window at all the passers-by and I enjoy my lovely long walks in the afternoons. In the evenings, Maisie and I like to snuggle up with Mum on the settee and watch TV. Oops – I forgot to mention how very much I love my food! A while back, Maisie and I had a falling out. Maisie was with her puppies and I was only trying to help out…..Maisie got scared and we had a big row about it. I went to stay at Grandma's until the pups had gone to their new homes. Afterwards, Maisie and I made up and have been like sisters ever since.

Every year Maisie and I go over to Ireland for a holiday for about 6 weeks. We go on a boat; it is called a 'ferry'. We run free over there and like seeing all the sheep and cows. We meet up with all the local dogs and when it's warm, all lie together on the village green. I love these holidays and love Mum for taking us.

November 2013

Maggie's owner: Linda Burden, Essex, England

QUIRKY THINGS THAT SCOTTIES DO

Does your Scottie.......

- ☐ Watch television?
- ☐ Jump up and bark at the TV when watching tennis, football, animals etc.?
- ☐ Sit at the window avidly watching the world go by?
- ☐ Lay with his/her head on your foot?
- ☐ Have an intense dislike of motorised vehicles?
- ☐ Have an intense dislike of anything with wheels – bicycles, scooters, roller skates, shopping trollies, wheelie bins...?
- ☐ Bark at the hoover/vacuum cleaner?
- ☐ 'Nose Butt' you when he/she wants something or wants you to do something?
- ☐ Have a particular attraction to feet and most items of footwear (including socks!)?
- ☐ Argue with the ironing board and then after, lay beside it chewing on the plastic coated feet?
- ☐ Believe he/she is a 'warrior' on a mission when out walking on a lead?
- ☐ Love to sleep on his/her back with feet in the air?
- ☐ After eating or drinking, simply have to wipe his/her beard clean and rub it dry on the nearest convenient (to them) surface, be it your furniture, carpet, door mat, lawn...?
- ☐ Like to follow the same route when out on a walk, even demanding to cross the road at the same place?

~~~

See how many boxes *your* Scottie ticks √ √

The Tourists

Featuring Madge, Pip and Peter Moore.   Photo by Lucy Moore

THE ELUSIVE SCOTTIE?

I rarely see another Scottie or meet one whilst out walking, on days out or on holiday. And so it has been my great pleasure to feature 68 Scotties in this book from various countries around the world.

The Scotties you have met in this book live in:

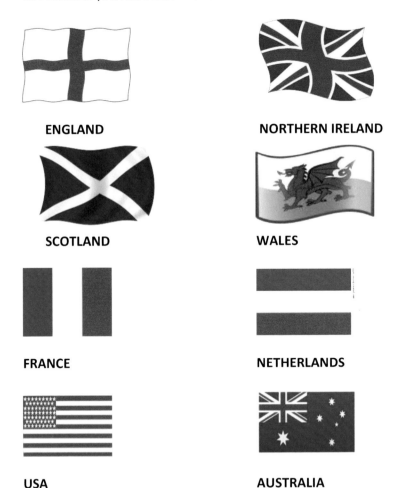

ENGLAND

NORTHERN IRELAND

SCOTLAND

WALES

FRANCE

NETHERLANDS

USA

AUSTRALIA

SCOTTIE GALLERY

'In Praise of Scotties' starred:

Molly and Bunty

Madge, Pip and Peter

Hamish and Holly

Freddie

Tucker

Hamish

Barney

Jock

Hamish

Andy, Hoanteg and Heather

Jazz and Beni

Lulu

Oscar

Jock   and

Maggie

Beth

Harry

Jock McPhee

Amy

Morag

Rosie

Bruce

Meg and Tessa

Striker

Pepper and Fala

Rody

Maeve, Murphy
and Maud

Corrado

Jock

Frazer

Pepper and Bonn

Jamie

Joc

Caspar

Alfie

Reggie and Bailey

William

Nessie

Jenson

Hamish, Bonny and Isla

Tink and Harley

Leonard

Rufus and Mishka

Jimmy and Jess

Pollyanna and puppies

Mac and Dougal

Nessie

Barley

Maggie

We hope you have

enjoyed this book

Murphy   Maud   Maeve

and thank you for supporting STECS

from

the Billingham Scotties

Index